REACH for Success

4 Strategies to Positively Impact Your Classroom

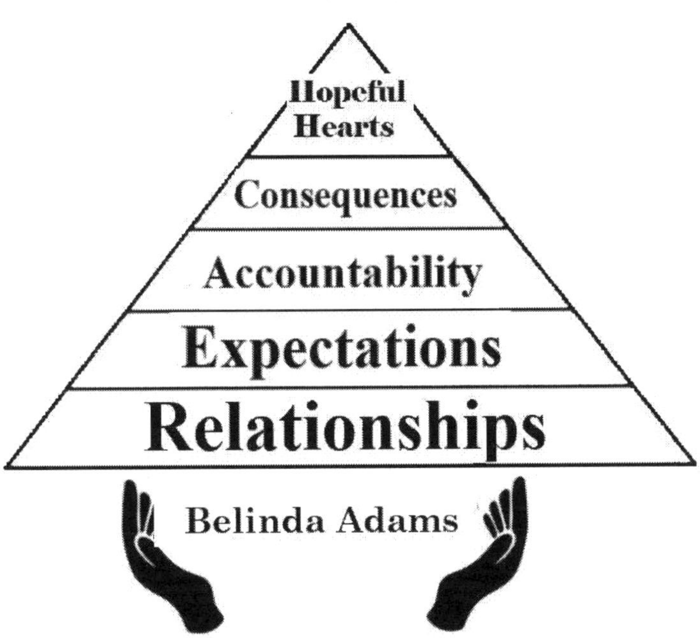

Belinda Adams

Award Winning Author of *Can You See Me?*

Anchor Book Press

REACH for Success

4 Strategies to Positively Impact Your Classroom

REACH for Success: 4 Strategies to Positively Impact Your Classroom

Imprint: Anchor Book Press
440 W Colfax Street, Unit 1132, Palatine, IL 60078
ISBN: 9781949109238
Printed in the United States

Dedication

This book is dedicated to educators across the globe who continually amaze me with their love and compassion for educating our youth!

What others are saying about Belinda Adams' books …

From her book, *Can You See Me?*

"Ms. Adams has a powerful message that many people, not just teachers, can benefit from. It will make you take a step back and think about how you can change and grow better as a person when faced with a challenge."

-Educator

"Just finished your book and sad that it's over. I want to read more. It was wonderful and I enjoyed it. Your humbleness in your successes and failures with these young minds is so uplifting.
Thank you for sharing your stories."

"Your book was exactly what I needed. I feel like the past two days with my class have been so great. I just needed that refresher of teaching with empathy and love.
I don't ever want to forget why I am here."

-Educator

"Just finished your story and loved it!!!
Well done and I hope it inspires others like it did me. It was educational to people like me that have no clue."

"Ms. Adams writes with her heart after discovering the difference that teaching with understanding makes. She gives practical ideas that are useful for ALL classrooms, but especially effective with children who have special needs and those living in poverty. As a former professor of teacher education, I recommend this book to all preservice teachers as teaching with understanding builds classroom success. Beginning teachers struggling for classroom control will also benefit from her tips for building a classroom based on mutual respect. Belinda Adams has learned and shares her tested protocols in an easy reading manner that will let you know that she feels your pain and wants to help you. I believe she CAN see you!"

-Professor

"We can learn much from others who find joy in what they do. In this book, Belinda Adams shares what it takes to not only be a teacher, but a leader to her students. Belinda has a vision that is greater than simply sharing knowledge with a student. She reminds us it is important to learn one's story and teach within that context. I look forward to reading the future books Belinda has already envisioned including reaching a student who has been impacted by trauma and saving a generation of "throw away kids."

-University Department Chair, Ph.D.

Foreward

Over the years of my teaching career, the work to complete became more and more time consuming. The demands placed upon educators by administration, both at the school level and the district level, continued to increase as a result of high-stake academic testing while student achievement decreased. Today teachers face many more challenges than I did when I began teaching over 20 years ago.

With these facts, I'd say that teachers today really have to have the mindset and the heart to successfully instruct young people. Without those two components, educators don't stand a chance of surviving. Either they burnout or find themselves terminated because they cannot meet the higher demands of the district.

For these reasons, I love Belinda Adam's new book, *REACH for Success.* It's a fast read (essential for time-challenged teachers) while providing concrete strategies that educators can quickly put into practice to experience the success that Belinda has had year after year in her own teaching career. For years, I watched Belinda work with students helping them find success, even those 'difficult kids' we all wanted to forget about. As I observed, I wondered why admin was not checking out the reason for her success. Did they realize what they were missing? Now we have the answer! Belinda has shared the strategies to her accomplishments in her new book, *REACH for Success.*

Teachers will find if they implement the concepts presented in *REACH for Success,* they will see the benefits for their students immediately. The foundation of *REACH for Success* is building relationships with your students; this concept is the footing that all the other concepts are built on. The good news is that most teachers start with relationships on day one. The bad news is that we tend to forget the importance as the school year progresses and demands increase. Belinda reminds us of the importance and suggests ways to continue the relationship building through the entire year.

Failure to lay the foundation may be one reason why educators throw their hands in the air and say, "I give up. This class is hopeless." If you ask Belinda, she'd say that "No class is hopeless! Every child wants to learn when they are provided with the right support and motivation. Developing positive relationships help students make sure their brains are available for learning."

Along this same line, being available, I think of the latest buzz word in education, growth mindset. While this is a great concept, many teachers are struggling as they find that it really isn't as easy as just telling a kid to change how he thinks. The reason is that hope is a prerequisite for growth mindset. Struggling students who have not experienced success are not going to be able to just change the way they think. In their experience, it just isn't true. They have no hope that life will ever be better. They have no hope that they can succeed. *REACH for Success* is the prerequisite we need to help students develop a growth mindset by helping develop hope.

Belinda's original REACH for Success model cannot be found in any book for education and classroom management. Yes, you might find a section on "Expectations" or "Importance of Developing Relationships." However, the REACH for Success model spells out the formula simply and logically in a way that guarantees student success. I have found through personal experience, when we leave out one of these critical components, our success rates plummet. It takes a little more time, but it is worth it – for our success as teachers, but more importantly for our students.

Join Belinda in her quest to find the inner learner in all of our students, to build classrooms that spark curiosity, and hope for the future.

Carol Pirog,
Author, Retired Educator

Table of Contents

Anchor Book Press

"Sometimes, what we do intuitively, as educators, to facilitate the process of learning using the path of least resistance is the best approach.

...Anytime it is within our power to do something for a child who is struggling, we should do it without hesitation."

Belinda Adams,
Don't Look Too Closely, 2018

Introduction

REACH for Success? You might be wondering what does it mean to "REACH for Success"? Let's be honest. If you're an educator, I'm sure you're working very hard - putting in those "extra" hours outside of your contractual time (be it grading papers, lesson planning, or brainstorming ways to engage your students in learning).

As educators, we are always *reaching*. Searching for ways to *reach* our students more effectively to get them engaged and keep them engaged. Planning for methods to *reach* the academic and personal growth goals we want for our students each year. And on some days, *reaching* deep inside ourselves for the resolve and resilience to continue to do what we do when we seem to be facing impossible odds.

Odds such as low student engagement, even lower student school readiness skills, and high administrative expectations. Most of the odds we face as educators are out of our control and can make our jobs even that much more frustrating. However, to be effective, we've got to remain positive! I've found the easiest way to remain positive against those and other impossible odds is to focus on what I (and you) can do to impact the factors we DO have control over – our classroom!

This book is a quick read, and hopefully, an eye-opening introduction to 4 strategies that can help you and your students *REACH* the success you are so desiring. If you notice, I didn't say 4 "easy" strategies because that wouldn't be realistic or reasonable. However, with practice, these strategies can become part of your teaching resources that are readily available for you to access.

It isn't by chance that the 4 key essential strategies for an effective classroom spell the word R-E-A-C-H. The triangle illustrates not only the order in which these elements should be introduced; the size of each section exemplifies its importance with regard to how successful your efforts will be.

Over the years, I've often asked my students, "Why is my class different than your other classes?" At the onset of the year, they're genuinely confused themselves because they haven't yet internalized or recognized what they are feeling about school. However, as the year goes by, and the question is repeated, my older students have said, "Because you make this a place where learning doesn't suck," and my younger students have said, "Because we have fun with the things we do in here!"

Without a doubt, most educators would dance themselves to the copy room for more copies of similar activities if these responses were common in their classroom. I ask myself, "Do I intentionally plan for lessons that don't 'suck'? Or am I trying to make all of my lessons fun?" The answer to that is a definite "no." However, I've found it's easier to engage students when the foundations have been securely established and even the mundane tasks take on new meaning for most students.

In this book, I will discuss the following strategies to build your ideal classroom, a classroom of students who come to your class ready to learn: R = relationships, E = expectations, A = accountability, C = consequences; all of which results in, H = hopeful students creating a happy classroom that's conducive to learning and growing. Let's get started!

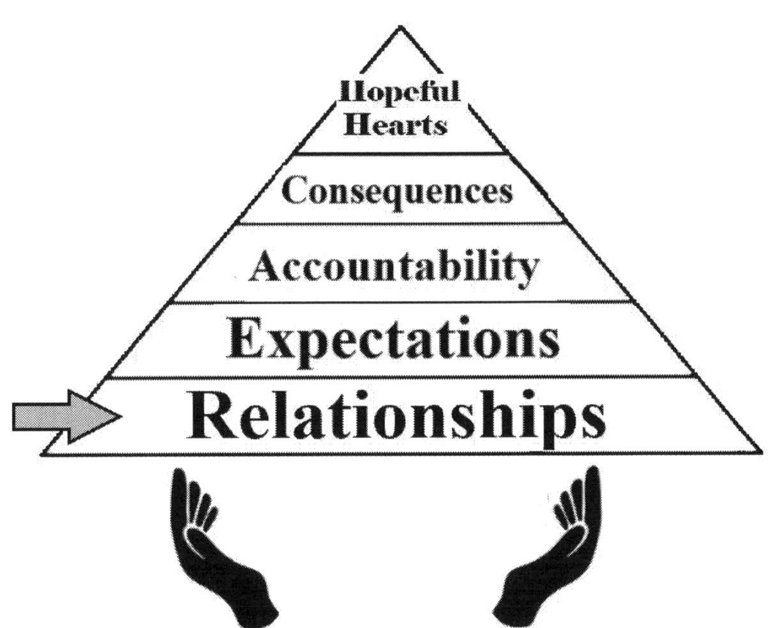
Hopeful
Hearts
Consequences
Accountability
Expectations
Relationships

Relationships

> *"If you don't have a relationship with your students, the work you do on a daily basis will be flat and not nearly as effective as what it could be."*
>
> *George & George, 2016*

Building relationships with students is instrumental in moving your students and classroom from merely a group of students to an effective, happy learning team. In my opinion, the best way to build relationships is to offer "openness" because openness between teacher and student builds trust, rapport, and lasting relationships. That's why the relationships portion of my diagram is the largest section. Without developing relationships with your students, everything else you do will be ineffective and more difficult.

Developing a relationship with your students is not as complicated as one might imagine, even with those students who work very hard to push you away. When I begin the process of building relationships, I like to consider approaches to accomplish the following:

- **Be real with your students.** Students need to view their teacher as a human being with a life and family beyond the walls of the school. It's important that we, as educators, share our personal stories at the beginning of the year and throughout the year. Just as we plan for those "beginning of the year activities" for the students to get to know one another and you to get to know them; teachers need to take the time and heart to share their personal stories as well. My younger students are astounded to discover that I have a family, a dog, and a house because, if you know many six-year-olds, they are convinced their teachers sleep behind their desks at night! My older students are often astounded to hear that their teacher became frustrated with traffic or forgot her lunch on the counter at home. (Yes, she IS human!) This approach is especially critical for my older students who have become accustomed to distancing themselves from the teachers who remain private about their lives outside of school. In this way, these students have already built in a prepared excuse in their minds to discount what the teacher has to say.

- **Be fallible in front of your students.** Teachers need to exhibit their "human side" – the mistakes we make, the dilemmas we face (as teachers, co-workers and parents). We need to be ready and humble enough to admit to our students when we make mistakes and how we plan to address it differently in the future. It's not as degrading as one might think.

Often, it's as simple as saying, "Hey guys, yesterday I got a little irritated when I didn't think you were following along with the lesson and I let you know about it … loudly. Maybe next time, if you guys will help me, we can take a few minutes to talk about how I can make the lesson more interesting or easier to follow. What do you think about that?" Or another example: "Friends, I know I seem a little flustered and short with you this morning, and I apologize. I had this great lesson planned, and when I got to school, the copier was broken and I couldn't get the copies done in time. Next time, I'm thinking I should probably make those copies the day before I plan to use them. I hope you can help me settle into learning this morning, and we will do that great activity tomorrow."

These approaches go a long way towards building lasting relationships where students trust you later on when you tell them they can complete a challenging task or encourage them when they fail time after time to master a skill.

- **Search for the gem in each student.** Students need to feel that their teacher can "see" their individual gifts and is aware of unique aspects about them. Maybe, one of them is great at sports, while another has a wonderful mind for mental math calculations, and still another has the voice of an angel. Let's be honest. Sometimes, a great deal of retrospection has to happen in order for the teacher to "find" the gem in certain students, especially those who seem to go out of their way to make our jobs more difficult. At times, I've had to talk with colleagues, and ask, "What can you tell me about Lauren?" in order for me to be able to see the "gem" I'm looking for. It's important for us to seek to "see" these gifts and to let the students know regularly that we see them. That way, they won't forget we know how special each and every one of them is, despite the challenges they bring. With regular reminders, students begin to polish and nurture that gem you see, and their self-confidence grows as well.

- **Look with a discerning eye at your students.** Teachers need to take the time to understand "where" each student is coming from with regard to how they feel about education. For example, I've discovered that many of my lower income students come from families who don't necessarily "value" education. That might be due to a variety of reasons, but regardless, it impacts how these students view education. When students come from this environment, they, too, might not see the value of education or grasp the point of excelling in academics because they cannot visualize any future for themselves that includes higher education. Not only do we need to understand where they stand on the value of education, we also need to make sure we acknowledge it. Let's not let it be the ugly elephant in the room. Let's say it out loud and bring the elephant into the light where we can talk about him. Again, this doesn't have to be a lengthy discussion. It can be as simple as saying, "You know, Johnny, I realize you don't see any reason to learn these concepts in math or complete your math work. I get that it's just not that important to you. You're not the only student I've had who felt that way. Can I tell you something? It is important, whether you realize it or not. And attempting to learn these concepts and letting me assist you will help both of us have a better day at school. What do you say you give that some thought?"

Other students may come from homes where "good" grades and high student achievement are stressed to the extent these students bring an increased level of anxiety with them to the classroom. These students, in my experiences, struggle with their need for perfection and are easily frustrated when asked to make corrections or do not receive the grade they (and their parents) are expecting. While I admit that I've often attempted to "educate" some parents on the value of learning, both achieved and failed attempts, I've also learned that these discussions can be one-sided and not in the best interest of the student. In these instances, I've determined it's best to prepare the student for life's lessons of failure, and attempt to show the student the worth of "failing" in order to become better at a certain task. It's not uncommon for me to comment: "If we succeed the first time at everything, what will happen when we later meet a challenge that's more difficult? We won't know how to respond. We've got to be prepared to face the challenge and do what is needed to get past it. That may mean extra effort on your part or simply asking for help when you need it."

- **Build a classroom sanctuary, a keystone to classroom success!** Finally, and most importantly in developing relationships is that teachers must cultivate a great classroom climate that includes the following …

    1. **Develop acceptance of one another** and acknowledge the talents (and challenges) of others. This classroom characteristic starts the first day of school with the get-to-know you activities that celebrate achievements and highlights interests. I think this leads right into the idea of building a classroom community and continues with the concept discussed below:

    2. **Build a feeling of community**. Send the message to your students that "community" isn't an option

for you and that it shouldn't be for them either. Let them know from Day 1 that you are "in it together". "Hey kiddos, we're all in this together for the next 175 days. Let's figure out how we can make these the best 175 days of our lives!" I'll give you a couple of examples. One year, I had a classroom layout that was just dreadful. I was sharing a room with another special education teacher with a wall divider down the middle that didn't even reach the ceiling or floor. The rectangular shape left little room for desks, let alone space for movement. Rather than trying to "hide" the challenges of the classroom layout, I laid it out there for the students and asked for suggestions. Our class spent the first several weeks rearranging furniture and supplies. The Principal often joked with them that she never knew what to expect when she walked into our classroom. Secretly, I think they found that pretty funny! As we neared the close of the first month of school, the students and I had "created" a classroom layout that worked for us (regardless of how others viewed it), and as I stood back and watched the students move from computers to the work table to their desks, I realized they were pretty darn impressed with what "they" had created. It was our room and one that made it conducive for them to learn! Another example: One year, our class had a student that all of the students (and yes, sometimes me as well) found very annoying. His habits of whining and asking questions I'd just answered often put all of the students on edge. I'd regularly look at the students, and make a "face," that they learned acknowledged how they were feeling about this particular student at that moment and sent my grateful acknowledgement of their patience to wait until he was done. By letting them discreetly know that I validated their feelings of being annoyed, yet showing I was still willing to listen to the student's questions or concerns, helped them understand the concept of respecting one another.

3. **Remember to give students "down time."** Whether it's 5 minutes to talk with their friends or neighbors at the beginning or end of class, or while you pretend to gather materials for the upcoming lesson or set up the SmartBoard. Or it's music you play each day at the same time of day or an opportunity for students to share a special talent, such as dancing or juggling (yes, I've had jugglers). All of these things are important to the overall environment you are striving to develop. In addition, with this approach, students learn there's a time for talking, dancing, juggling, laughing, and a time for settling into learning. That balance, and distinction, encourages the

perseverance of learning when they know there's going to be time for those other things, as well.

4. **Add humor and fun every day!** Maybe it's a funny story a student wants to share. Maybe it's a ridiculous thing you did, either personally or at school. I was infamous for having students line up too early for a special, and then having to send them back to their seats, or forgetting it was early dismissal and being genuinely surprised when lunch came at 10:25 in the morning! My favorite story of my genuine theatrics was the day one of my bracelet charms become lodged in the latch hole on my computer keyboard. I was literally attached to my computer! Rather than pretend it wasn't happening, I called one of the students over and had the "engineer" of the group take a look. Quite certainly, he couldn't contain his astonishment (and amusement) and had to call a few other students over to take a look. Before I knew it, all of them were gathered around the computer, each throwing out a suggestion for this problem. When the teacher next door heard the commotion, she stuck her head around the divider and said, "What's going on?" I let the "engineer" explain, and follow it up with his own hypothesis of needing a screwdriver to take the computer apart. After everyone finished with a round of laughter, the teacher approached and said, "Before

we do any of that, how about we have Mrs. Adams take off the bracelet? Then, we can determine our next steps." Well, how come I hadn't thought of that?! This is still a story shared by teachers, students, and the computer technician whenever the opportunity presents itself. I was happy to have the problem solved and even happier the students, fellow teacher, and I had enjoyed a good laugh!

Whatever it might be, be sure to find something for you and the students to laugh about together. It's important and goes a great distance towards developing the relationship that encourages students to want to work for you and do their best to achieve success.

Questioning - A Keystone to Building Student Relationships

"...Questions ignite great conversations about future learning and behavior. ...Demonstrating to students their own ability to turn the uninteresting into the interesting, and yes, even have fun in the process - is invaluable." (Maiers, 2012, p. 46).

Ways to Foster Questioning:

Let me preface this section by acknowledging that questions can often be like a double-edge sword when viewed as a disruption and nuisance. Teachers who feel especially pressured to maintain a schedule of curriculum pacing and lesson completion are often especially bothered by the interruption of questions. In order to address that first, I propose the following strategy:

- **Utilize a "post-it, park-it" board** at the door of the classroom and provide students with a stack of post-its. Students who have "burning" questions should feel encouraged to quickly write down their question and put it on the "parking lot" right away. This strategy can also be helpful for the shy students. In this way, those students who have questions can ask them without feeling put on the spot or embarrassed in the event the other students find their question "dumb". This is a fantastic tool as long as you make sure you get to those questions and answer them.

Plan for a certain time of day when those questions are addressed, either for the class as a whole or individually if necessary. Be aware that students will catch on quickly if you disregard the questions they wrote and you'll lose some respect and credibility along the way.

- **Allow questions at any time.** It's okay to ask students if you can get back to them at a later time when you are finished with the task at hand. Most often, they will agree to hold onto the question. However, be prepared that if they can't; you might have to detour for a few minutes to answer that burning question.

Let me share a humorous story about allowing questions at any time. During my years of teaching 5th grade, I had a particularly challenging group of students who soon became my favorite group because of their tenacity to challenge me to be a better teacher by engaging them. They loved (and needed) to be told the "why" of the lesson and "how" they were going to use it once they learned it. They never got tired of hearing that, and it encouraged me to dig deeper for meaningful lessons because I knew they would ask the why and how.

One of the girls was from a low-income apartment complex near the school, and she had developed a rough exterior in order to protect herself from the elements of that environment. This often made it difficult for me to engage her. That was, until she discovered, she really liked my apparel! One day, during the middle of a principal's observation for my evaluation, she raised her hand and said she had a question. After I said, go ahead, she proceeded to say, "Girlfriend ... I am in love with those shoes! Can you tell me later where you got them?" After I stifled a smile (as I could see my observer was doing the same), I let her know that I appreciated her compliment and I'd be glad to share the information about where I got the shoes once we got into our small groups. She responded, "Cool," and we got back to the lesson. Another example is the student who "always" had a question, each and every day! As the year progressed, I was able to get him to "hold" onto that burning question of the day until he came to his small group rotation, but I always had to be prepared for when he said, "Yeah, but this just can't wait!" If that happened to be the case, I had to be prepared to detour for a few moments, answer the question with the shortest explanation, and promise more detailed information when he came to small group. (This strategy also kept that student engaged with learning as he was anticipating our discussion when he came to small group.)A win-win for us both! In these cases, and others like them, allowing questions builds relationships in the classroom that cannot be developed any other way than through sharing and openness.

"If our classrooms remain places where curiosity is nurtured, developed and celebrated, the gift we give our students extends beyond the classroom walls." (Maiers, p. 55)

Sense of Community – A Second Keystone to Building Student Relationships

"The skills of building relationships, learning and working on teams, communicating, managing conflicts, and setting personal goals … are better preparation for succeeding in the real world than sitting silently through 2-hour standardized testing." (Benson, 2014, p. 135)

Remember the boy the class found annoying and whiney? One day, during lunch recess, a group of students from another class were "picking" on this particular student, calling him names like "baby," "whiny," and "mama's boy." When I discovered later that my students stuck up for him and told the other students to "back off," I asked why they had defended our student. (Of course, I asked this when the student left the room to go to the bathroom.) They replied, "Well, we might think he's annoying and a pain to be around, but he's from our classroom and we stick together," That's community!

I make a conscious effort to never miss an opportunity to tell a class as a whole why I like them.

I've had students ask, "Are we the best class you've ever had?" I usually answer with that one statement that sums up who they are as a group. For example, I might say, "Yep, you are the best class I've ever had at figuring out new ways to learn math" or "You know what? You are the class that makes me laugh the most. We have a lot of fun in here!" Making sure I describe why they are the "best" is much different than simply responding "yes." It's the same concept used when providing a student or group of students with a compliment. Few want to hear "good job". They want to hear, "Good job at finishing that VENN diagram with such detail" or "Great job at sticking with that assignment because it was a challenge and you did it!" Even the youngest of students can discern the difference between what I call "empty compliments" such as "good job" from the compliments that truthfully makes a statement about them as a group or individuals.

Every class has a climate. You can build it and cultivate it. Or it will develop on its own. Keep in mind, climate developed on its own sometimes results in a less productive atmosphere than you were hoping for.

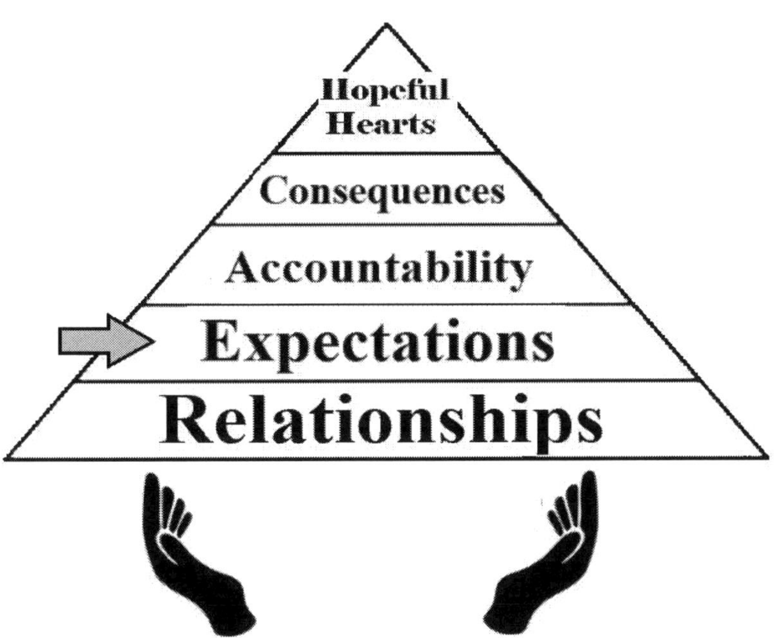
Hopeful
Hearts
Consequences
Accountability
Expectations
Relationships

Expectations

I think, many times, as educators, we assume that students disobey the rules because they choose to. And, in some instances, this is very true. What we cannot lose sight of is the fact that many students come to school without a clue of what is "expected" of them as a student. In these situations, we've got to teach them explicitly, model frequently, and reinforce positively when we see success.

Belinda Adams,
Author/Educator

Expectations are important in defining what will and will not be acceptable for your classroom. It's also imperative that students have a role in developing the classroom expectations. In this way, you can achieve "buy in" from the students and increase the chance of the students consistently following the classroom expectations.

You might wonder how I define "expectations." Prior to my third year of teaching, I referred to them by what most teachers call them: "rules." However, most students, and especially those who come from homes with little to no rules, classroom rules become another way to alienate them from the classroom environment. And let's be honest, many of the rules students face at school seem arbitrary and unnecessary. "Don't run in the hallways" (except when you're about to miss the bus and your teacher tells you to). "Keep silent in the hallways" (unless the principal starts asking you about your day and you are encouraged to answer). See what I'm getting at? A lot of the rules we enforce at school really seem hypocritical to our students and pretty much useless.

Therefore, just the mere mention of "classroom rules" in my classroom can often cause many students to push the "tune out the teacher" button. If this happens, teachers will not receive buy in, and these same students will be intent upon not following the classroom rules simply because of the label.

When my students and I discuss expectations, I explain it as simply as possible. Expectations are guidelines that we can expect from one another so that our class can "live" together in the same room and get some learning done.

One expectation every student is eager to buy into is the expectation that everyone has a chance to speak. In order for that to be the case, it's important that students raise their hand and wait to be called on so that everyone has a chance to speak and students are not talking over one another. What student doesn't want to be heard? Usually, this is an expectation everyone is willing to accept. It really matters how a concept is presented to the students. In this case, it can be presented as something you cannot do (talk without raising you hand) or something you can do (have the chance to be heard). When students view expectations as "can do" actions rather than "can't do" actions, the mere distinction changes how they view the expectation as a whole. If you think about the classroom expectations listed on the following page, try to see each from the viewpoint of a student. Rather than telling students they can't get out of their seats, it's a matter of "everyone can get out of their seats when they raise their hand and let me know." Might be a minor difference to you and I, but in the mindset of a student who feels besieged by school rules, these small distinctions make a world of difference.

It's easy to overlook the division made above with the approach of those expectations. Rather than making it about the irritation and chaos caused by talking out without raising a hand (definitely the underlying truth about why we ask for and expect students to raise their hands before talking); instead the discussion becomes about giving every student an opportunity to talk and be heard by the teacher and his or her peers. Instead of having a discussion about students running into one another walking around or disrupting the lesson by moving around, the conversation settles on the reason the student needs to leave their seat. These small differences can often change the perception of the students in accepting the classroom expectations.

Over the course of my teaching career, with the help of my students, and guiding them through the process, I've narrowed our classroom expectations to resemble the following:

1. Show you are ready for learning by being in your seat ready to learn.
2. Raise your hand to speak or to ask to get out of your seat.
3. Listen for directions and follow them when asked the first time.
4. Keep hands, feet, objects, and hurtful words to yourself.
5. Let us help you when you need help.

To reinforce the classroom expectations for my younger students (Grades K, 1 & 2), I've developed the practice of reading a classroom "social story" at the beginning of each day. Yes, it's the same story every day. You might wonder if the students complain about the repetition, and I can honestly say, they do not. I remind them that, by reading our social story, I am giving them the "key" to a great day. "It's almost like someone giving you the answers to a test." That really gets their attention! I've found it helpful to color code each page so that I begin the expectation, and they finish it with the words that are colored. It's a great way to "get everyone on the same page" for learning. One day, the principal asked my students why we read the social story every morning, and they replied, "It's just what we do to get our day off to a good start!" For older students, it may only be necessary to revisit the story after school breaks or if behavior becomes challenging to manage. Sample pages from my morning social story are located in the Resources section at the back of the book.

You might wonder how do expectations impact student growth and learning? A great deal, I would answer. So many of our students come to school without the school readiness skills they need to be successful. Not all of them were taught at home that you wait your turn to talk or that it's not appropriate to disrupt the learning of others by yelling or throwing things when you are frustrated. Not having been taught these expectations, receiving daily reinforcement at school helps students to develop learning fortitude to stick with it, even when it gets difficult.

Using If/Then Statements

Using If/Then statements are a great way to explain your expectations to all students, especially those who struggle with hearing several directions using too many words. Students who clearly understand the If/Then statements are more likely to follow directions and meet the expectations because they understand undoubtedly what will happen when an expectation is followed.

If/Then charts can be used in a variety of ways. Some educators use them to also explain consequences. I have found over the years that most students view "If/Then" statements about consequences as a threat, and many trying students may view those statements as a challenge or opportunity to engage in a power struggle with the adult stating the expectation. A sample "If/Then Statement" chart can be found in the Resources section.

Options for other types of statements that can be used to clearly explain Consequences rather than the If/Then statements will be discussed later in the book.

Set Students Up for Success

Many times, students fail to meet expectations because of frustrations. To help manage this, educators need to plan "how" to support our students - academically and emotionally. It's much easier to assist students with their frustrations when students are taught how to share the fact that they *are* frustrated in appropriate ways and *how* to ask for help. This concept circles back to relationships. If you have shared your own mistakes and frustrations and demonstrated how to ask for help (maybe you've asked them or they've heard you ask another teacher), then you have already set the stage for students to ask for help naturally. Remember, the younger the students, plan on many, many reminders and re-modeling of this behavior because frustrations in younger children can often be expressed in disruptive and inappropriate ways. Further, older students who have had negative previous school experiences and/or do not have positive role models at home, may need to be reminded of the appropriate way to express frustrations that limit the disruption to the class and facilitates them in receiving the assistance they need.

> Reminder to self and other educators: "…don't let your high expectations limit your students and what they can accomplish. …Often our perception of what they can accomplish limits them, even when they are set at high levels. … Push the students and they will surprise you … and you might surprise yourself."
>
> (George and George,2016, http://inservice.ascd.org/author/admin)

I had a student once who joined my classroom after a very negative year in first grade. He had learned that, if his behavior was bad enough, he would be sent home. Being sent home "worked" for him because he was able to avoid the unpreferred tasks, such as reading and writing.

A few months into the school year, after hearing me explain repeatedly that I wasn't sending him home because of his behavior, he began to buy into the idea that expectations allowed him to experience less stress and anxiety because he knew what he was supposed to be doing … at all times! One day, on a particularly emotional day, he began to act out. I utilized the If/Then concept when speaking to him, saying, "Tony, if you continue to disrupt the class with your negative behavior, then you will need to remove yourself from the instructional area so the rest of your friends can work." I also took that opportunity to remind him, "Even if you choose to continue this behavior, this will not result in you being sent home. He responded, "Yeah, I know, I know! I'm not going home. We will just have to work this out at school."

For students who respond to structure and routine, expectations provide them with the security of knowing how they should respond and function in the classroom. It's also important that they know and understand the consequences ahead of time. In this way, students have the opportunity to decide on their own about their behavior prior to breaking a classroom expectation. Students, like this one, who previously used school suspension as motivation for misbehavior, learned that his behavior had an expectation and it provided a framework for him to understand the change from his previous school experiences.

A Classroom Expectations Chart I designed and utilize for my classroom can be found in the Resources section at the back of the book.

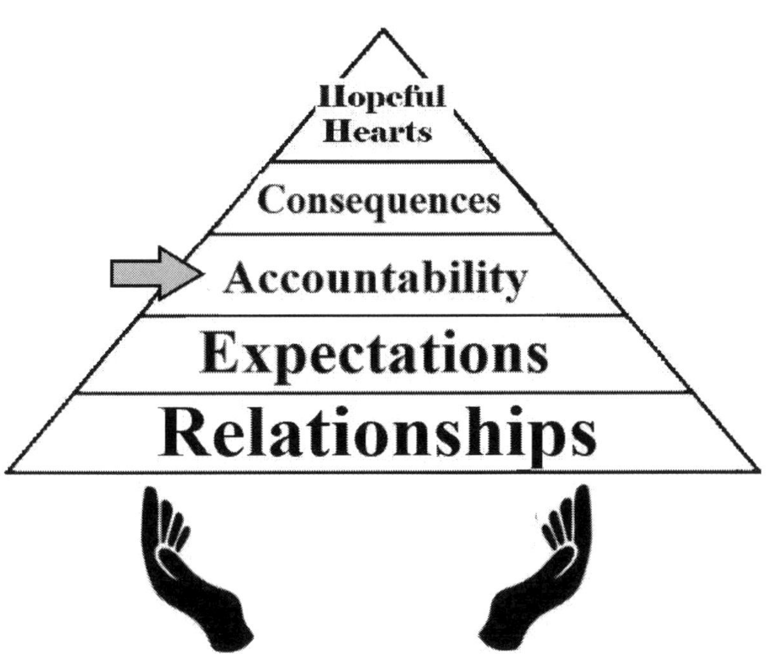
Hopeful
Hearts
Consequences
Accountability
Expectations
Relationships

Accountability

"It's amazing how much the student's perception plays into the success or failure of a strategy. When students have a perception of control over a given situation, they are more likely to follow teacher directives. When students perceive they have no control, and are expected to bend under coercion, the teacher and the students will find themselves in a power struggle. No one wins in a power struggle."

Belinda Adams,
If Only She Knew, 2019

I have found over the course of my teaching career that the one element that is often missing in the classroom culture is the concept of accountability. A lot of times, it is the same classrooms where accountability is missing that teachers complain of misbehavior, lack of respect, and classrooms that are ineffective.

I define "accountability" as being completely responsible for what you do and being able to provide a satisfactory reason for doing the action or not doing an action. Accountability ties hand in hand with expectations. Without holding students accountable for meeting or not meeting the classroom expectations, the expectations themselves become meaningless.

Students respond well to prompts of being held accountable through "friendly reminders" of the expectations in the classroom and their responsibility to be part of the learning process. In this way, the students feel like they are part of a "team" of learners and take ownership for their behaviors and actions.

The morning social story is one simple way of reminding students of the classroom expectations. It's your way of letting them know that, now that they know them, you are holding them accountable to complete the expected tasks or behaviors. Students learn quickly that you are giving them a great deal of responsibility and often respond in ways that surprise you.

It's also important to acknowledge the student's reason for not following the expectation in the first place. One complaint I've often heard from disgruntled students is that "teachers just don't listen." By acknowledging the student's reason or explanation for not following the expectation, the teacher isn't agreeing with the student. Instead, the teacher is validating the student's reason and repeating it back to assure him that he was heard.

A simple phrase I often use might be: "Juan, I am sorry that you feel this work is a waste of time;

however, the expectation is that you complete the work just like the rest of the class. I'll check back with you in three minutes and you can let me know how I can help you do that." That statement acknowledges Juan's feelings and restates the expectation with accountability involved. You can then follow up with the consequence if the student needs additional reminders. Consequences will be discussed in the next section of this book.

Another example is, "Rebekah, I'm sorry you're feeling tired today after a long weekend. It's unfortunate that you got to bed late. However, you do know that even though you're tired, we've got work to do and I know you can get it done. Remember, there will be an opportunity for free time later today if we can get our work completed. I'll check in with you in 5 minutes to see how you are doing." Simple, straight-forward comments such as these let students know you are holding them accountable for the work they are expected to do while at the same time communicates your willingness to assist them with the work if they need help.

Students, even my youngest students, respond well to this approach, and seem to work harder to complete the task if they feel you understand their reservations for doing the work. In addition, just like the rest of us who work for a reward (our paycheck), students need to be reminded that when they meet the expectations, they will earn a preferred activity, even if it's a 5-minute sensory break after completing the work.

One way teachers can assure the student you are ready to deliver on your promise of a preferred activity when class work is complete is to have the students complete an "Interest Survey." An Interest Survey can be found in many presentations on lots of websites and printable materials. I like to create my own Interest Survey because I can align the possible preferred activities with the activities I find acceptable for my group of students (which can change from year to year depending upon the students I have). The Interest Survey really boils down to one question you want the student to determine: "What am I willing to work for?" For students who haven't had an opportunity to think about this concept before, it also allows them the chance to explore their own interests and settle on what they *are* willing to work for. Teachers also need to be prepared that a student's preferred activity/task may change as the year progresses, so it might be necessary to conduct the Interest Survey more than once a year. A sample copy of an Interest Survey I developed can be found in the Resources section of this book.

Let me share a story of a student of mine who truly defines the need for accountability. Jake was a student who never really completed any class work.

He would sit quietly looking down at his paper, and because he was quiet about it, his lack of engagement often went unnoticed. When it was time to transition to another subject, he would quickly put the unfinished work into his desk and look ready to get started on the next activity. About 2 weeks into school, it came to my attention that I had no grades to add to my grade book under Jake's name.

The next morning, before school began, I looked inside Jake's desk. To my amazement, I found two weeks' worth of class work crammed inside. As I pulled each out, I saw that some had been started, but surprisingly, not one of them had been completed.

That morning, I paid particular attention to what Jake was doing during work time. With disbelief, I saw that he *really* wasn't doing anything. Quietly, I approached him and squatted down beside his desk. "Is there a problem with the class work?" Quiet pause. "Is there something I can explain to help you get started?" Now, the disbelief was on his face as he realized I was "on to" his habit of incomplete work. He could not find the words to answer.

After giving him a minute to respond and still receiving no answer, I told him I'd like to talk with him after class. With resignation, he nodded his head. I'm sure Jake was expecting a lecture about his incomplete work, a threat to call home to his mother, and a reminder that he would be failing my class. Instead, I began with, "I feel like I haven't done a good enough job explaining how to do the class work for you. I wish you would have told me that I needed to step up my game because that might have helped me realize I needed to explain it better so you could finish your work." Again, this poor boy was speechless because, as we both knew, that wasn't the reason his work was incomplete.

After looking at me incredulously for about 30 seconds, he found the words to respond saying, "Mrs. Adams, it ain't you that's the problem. It's just I don't really see the point. We just do more work after work, and I know I ain't learning nothing anyway." When I asked how he was so certain he knew he wasn't learning anything, he said he wasn't sure why he felt that way, but that's how he felt.

Jake and I made an agreement that day. Rather than allowing him to continue to sit and not do his work, I would remind him each day that I was expecting him to do it (because I knew he could!) and I would hold him accountable for completing it. He asked, "What's that? Is that where you call my mom if

I don't do it?" I answered, "No, it's letting you know that I am going to notice if you do your work, and I'm going to help you when you need it, and make sure it gets done. If you don't do the work, then we will have to talk about the consequences of that choice, but I'm sure we can make it happen together, without the consequences." "Oh," was all he had to say as he headed off to lunch.

My observation and acknowledgement of Jake doing his class work seemed to make all the difference for him. No longer did he sit at his desk doing nothing. He raised his hand for help when he needed it, and surprised himself with the work he was able to complete independently when he applied himself.

Another strategy I've used to assist students on their journey of academic independence is to provide them with a checklist (either on their desk or located in a handy folder). The checklist includes questions that assist the student in helping himself before asking for help from the teacher. Holding those students with a checklist accountable for using the checklist is very important. Before answering any questions from a student, it's imperative to ask, "Have you looked at your checklist? Have you gone through questions 1, 2 and 3? When you've done that, raise your hand, and I will be happy to help you?" An example of a student checklist can be found in the Resources section.

Returning to Jake, you might wonder if my reminders of accountability helped him complete his work every day? I won't lie to you and answer emphatically "yes" because, as with most of our students, every day are two words that shouldn't be part of our vocabulary. Students are young people. They're still learning to be available to learn and learning how to build upon what they already know to develop higher skills. To expect students to meet our expectations every day would certainly lead us all down the road of disappointment. Instead, I call it a victory for Jake and myself when Jake was able to complete his work more days than he didn't. That was definitely a step in the right direction considering he was previously completing no work.

The Delicate Balance between Too Little and Too Much Support

Throughout this section, I've mentioned several times the need to provide students with expectations, let them know you are holding them accountable and provide them with a level of support.

Many times, I've seen teachers providing students with a level of support that is too much, often completing the classwork for them. Just as many times, I've witnessed teachers push students into frustration and shut down mode by assuming they do not need any level of support and expecting them to complete classwork completely on their own. I've even heard teachers say they have already explained it to the class, they are not explaining it again for one student who wasn't listening.

It's invaluable that you gain students' trust when they believe you are holding them accountable for what you KNOW they can do! In other words, you are meeting every student where they are academically and emotionally able to complete the work (with assistance as needed). Meeting students where they are, rather than planning the same work for every student, lets students know you are aware of their strengths and weaknesses. Further, providing the appropriate level of support encourages independence and fosters confidence. Students move forward as they gain additional skills, and teachers can begin to lessen the level of support they are providing for each student.

Yes, at times, it becomes necessary for teachers to "push" that reluctant learner to challenge him academically; however, it's important to recognize when the student is no longer working because he is incapable of doing the work expected. Pushing students too soon for work independence with too little support can cause some students to shut down in frustration or embarrassment at their lack of abilities. It's also important to recognize the student who is "milking" his teacher for all of the assistance he can get in order to do as little work as possible independently. This is certainly a delicate balance, but I believe it comes easier and easier as teachers "tune into" the individual strengths and weaknesses of each student.

Levels of Support to increase academic independence:

- **Instruct students to use wall resources.** These resources might include the checklist I discussed earlier, word walls, and step-by-step flow charts.

- **Determine a student's level of independence.** I've had students who began the school year with so little confidence that he or she needed to work at my small group table (even when I wasn't working with that particular student). Students often feel a level of "safety" that help is close by and this proximity gives them the impetus to complete the work. I've had other students who started independent work with the understanding that he or she could raise a hand when they had completed 1 problem to have it checked by the teacher. Teachers who utilize this approach can increase the number of problems the student is required to complete as they gain confidence to encourage more independence. This approach can also be used with a visual timer where students are told they can return to the work table to have their work checked in 5 minutes. Not only does this encourage the student to get some work completed in that 5-minute period, but it also gives them accountability to complete the work.

- **Increase workload and/or increase increments** of time or problems between "check-ins" as students become more confident. Teachers need to be mindful that students may slide back and forth on the appropriate level of support as you begin new units or the student struggles in a particular area of instruction, such as math.

I think sometimes teachers consider expectations and accountability as the same concept when, in reality, they mean two completely different things. Accountability is simply the fact that a person/student will be responsible for their work. And in the classroom, accountability happens when students know the teacher will be checking on their progress and reminding them that it is a classroom expectation that they are responsible for their work. The teacher's job is to hold students accountable – verify that expectations are being met and providing support where needed. Students notice, and in more cases than not, they rise to the challenge.

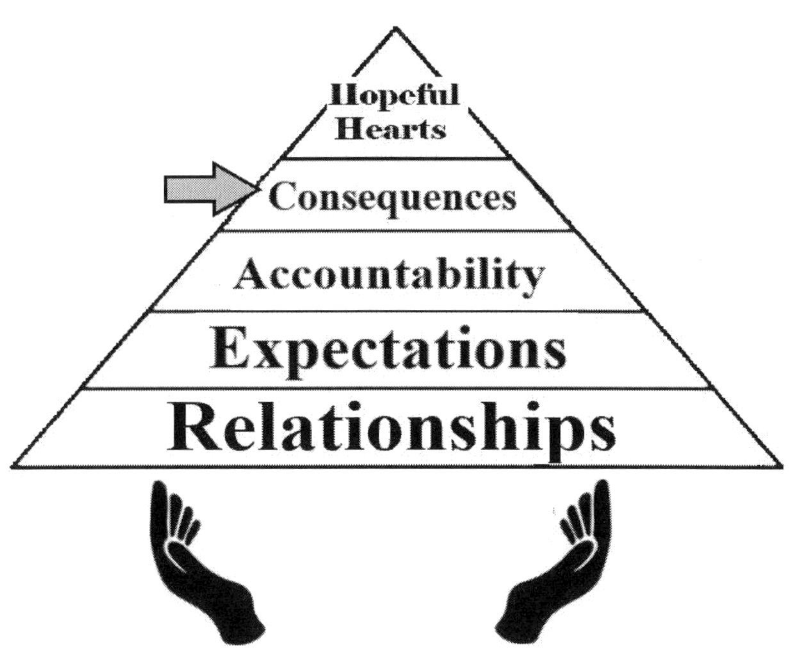
Hopeful
Hearts
Consequences
Accountability
Expectations
Relationships

Consequences

"Consequences are probably the best tool to use in our quest to internalize controls."
Fay & Funk, 1995

Consequences are the actions which occur when students do not meet the classroom expectations, be it with behavior or not completing their work. In many classrooms, consequences are referred to as "punishments," another word I omitted from my school vocabulary about the third year of teaching.

The word "punishment" has such a negative connotation. And far too often, teachers impose punishments that are not related to the infraction. In this case, punishments are seen negatively by the student. Further, many students take no steps toward learning so that they can avoid the punishment by changing their behavior in the future. These students simply hate school because of punishments that seem arbitrary and random without making the connection between their behavior and the punishment. It's been my experience that punishments can also lead to power struggles between the teacher and students.

I've experienced that students perform best in the classroom when the consequences are a natural outcome of the expectation which was not followed. It can be as simple as, "If you don't complete the math page now, you will have to complete it some other time during the day, and it may have to happen during a preferred activity. However, the math page has to be done."

In addition, my students have responded most positively to consequences that are predictable, no surprises. Usually, when we discuss the classroom expectations and come to agreement upon them, we discuss the consequences of not following them at the same time. In this way, students know up front what the consequence for their actions will be. Definitely, students (especially younger ones) require frequent reminders of the consequences. By providing reminders, students have a higher tendency of not becoming angry when the consequence occurs and cannot say, "I didn't know that was what was going to happen."

One classroom consequence for my students is that a student who continues to disrupt the learning of others over the course of several hours spanning consecutive days will spend a number of hours in the principal's office doing their work. In this way, the students learn that, when they disrupt the class, they lose the privilege of being part of class. And yes, I use the word "privilege" with the students, reminding them that being part of the classroom is something they earn with behavior that follows our classroom expectations. It's even better if the student being removed from class feels he is going to miss out on a great lesson or activity! (If sending the student to work in the office is not an option for you, partner with another teacher and agree to take each other's students when a student needs time out of the class.) Reminder: this is only effective if you've developed those relationships and classroom climate that makes the classroom a desirable place from the start.

An example of this would be the year I had a 1st grader named Joey, who unfortunately, had an inclination to throw his pencil, tear his paper and disrupt the rest of the class when he became frustrated with his work. After several instances of losing a preferred activity time with no change in behavior, the principal and I decided to increase the consequence. We let Joey know ahead of time that, the next time he disrupted the class from learning, he would have to lose time out of the classroom and do his work in the Principal's office. So, Joey was well aware of what would happen if he chose this behavior in the future. It didn't take long for Joey to experience this consequence.

One morning, after a particularly rough afternoon the previous day, Joey was escorted to the

Principal's office with his work and stationed at a small table in her office. At first, he worked diligently at the class work in front of him. However, soon, he started to become agitated and, at one point, ran from her office, making a beeline to our classroom door, all the while yelling over his shoulder, "I can't get an education in here! I've got to get back to my classroom right now!"

When Joey appeared at my door followed by an out of breath Principal, I quietly took his hand and led him back to the Principal's office and sat him in the chair. When he started crying and rubbing his eyes saying, "I can't do this, Mrs. Adams! I thought I could, but this is just too much consequence. Can't I come back to class now? I promise I won't bother the class anymore." Even though my resolve was slipping a little, I quietly held up my arm and pointed to my watch, drawing Joey's attention away from crying. I asked if he could read the time and he did. I told him, "You have 52 minutes left until your consequence is over. This is how much time you lost yesterday in the classroom instead of learning. I know you can do 52 more minutes, don't you? After your time is finished, you can return to the class for the rest of the day. I'll be waiting for you to come back."

Yes, Joey was able to complete his consequence, and returned to the class, looking more relieved than ever to be in the classroom! He learned a valuable lesson about "earning" the privilege to stay in the classroom with his peers by not disturbing their work. He also learned, quite hilariously, that you just can't get an education in the principal's office.

Another example would be students who refuse to be productive when given assignments on the computer or Chromebook. I've had many students who find this type of assignment boring and often allow their minds and eyes to wander away from the work in front of them. With today's increased use of technology, not only in the classroom but in every workplace, learning to maintain focus during computer time is a skill that must be mastered if we expect our students to be successful in their future careers. Those same students who find assignments "boring" often become very animated when allowed to play games or other activities on the computer. One consequence for students who consistently fail to accomplish their computer work is that they lose the privilege of using their computer for a period of time. Instead, work is printed for them. When the rest of the students are logging onto their computer, I quietly place the "independent work folder" on their desk and walk away. (When dealing with defiant or precocious students, I've placed their computer out of reach and out of sight.) When other students are having the opportunity to engage in free time activities on the computer, that student is given the option to draw or complete word puzzles at his seat. It's amazing how quickly students are ready to try those computer assignments again!

Additionally, we've got to be mindful that consequences do not have to be punitive to be effective. Sometimes, we can utilize simple consequences to provide students an opportunity to return to the learning environment and move on with their day. For example, I have a "Quiet Area" at the back of my classroom. I have strategically placed some small posters in this area describing what students can do or think about while they are there. One poster reads, "How am I feeling? What do I need to get ready for learning?" Another poster states, "Taking deep breaths is one way I can calm my body and get ready for learning." I also have a small (inexpensive) 2-minute timer in this area. Students respond very well to a liquid timer which they turn over and watch for the colored fluid to go to the bottom. It was a great coincidence that the liquid takes 2 minutes to settle. Please note that I mentioned the word "inexpensive" above because it's important to remember that some escalated students may initially use their time at the Quiet Area in destructive ways. An inexpensive timer allows them to be easily replaced and teaches the students that you're committed to the process.

At the onset of the school year, students need to be instructed about what they can do in the Quiet Area in order to return to the class activity. And that expectation can be repeated when the direction is given. For example, "Rhonda, I'd like you to take 2 minutes in the Quiet Area. You can use that time to think about what other choices you can make next time instead of blurting out the answers" or "Mikey, please go to the Quiet Area to calm down and use that time to breathe. When you're ready to join the class and follow the expectations, raise a quiet hand and let me know." By utilizing this strategy, students do not see the Quiet Area as a punishment; instead, they view it as a way that I am helping them get back on track and return to the class lesson or discussion.

In Teaching with Love and Logic, Fay & Funk point out that, "The effective teacher administers consequences with empathy and understanding, as opposed to anger and lecture." (p. 36)

Remember Joey's story about "too much consequence"? By telling him that I understood how he was feeling, he knew I was empathizing with him. My actions and words demonstrated that I was not angry with him and his consequence was not meant as hurtful. In this way, Joey took ownership of the consequence as a result of his behavior. Hopefully, Joey also internalized the idea that, by controlling his responses to frustration, he could remain in the classroom with his peers.

Consequence + Empathy = Learning
(Fay & Funk, 1995)

In Teaching Children to Care, author Charney agrees: "Consequences make the boundaries and limits clear. They preserve the safety of the individual student and of the community. It is critical that children know what happens when they fail to help themselves and the negative behavior occurs." (Charney, p. 357).

Teachers can become very creative with logical consequences that are not seen as punitive by the students. The Quiet Area is one example. Another example might be writing a note of apology to a student who may have been mean or disrespectful to another student or staff member. Still another example might be requiring the student to stay and help restack the library books she knocked over while not following the expectations while the rest of the class returns to the classroom. It's amazing what they think they're missing in the 5 minutes it takes for them to help clean up.

Being creative and logical with consequences is an essential part of developing consequences that are meaningful to your students. You might need to get to know them, their particular likes and dislikes, before you can develop consequences that accomplish the goal you have in mind of deterring future misbehavior. This is the key to effective consequences – your goal must be to change behavior, not punish student for poor choices.

In addition to finding creative and logical consequences, educators can also discuss with students that consequences do not always have a negative connotation. For example, I often give students a choice of a consequence. Students begin to see that, although consequences are a necessary outcome of their behavior, they also provide them with some options. Consequences stated in this way show students that their teacher is not using the "My way or the highway" approach to classroom management.

An example of using choices for consequences might be asking the student what they feel might be an acceptable consequence for not meeting classroom expectations. Another example might be to offer the student a choice, such as, "You have not completed your morning work as expected, you can either (1) complete this work during a preferred activity, or (2) I can send it home as homework with the understanding that if it is not completed and returned tomorrow morning, you will have to complete it during a preferred activity."

In my experience, most of my students would rather complete the work while they are still at school because they don't want to have homework. However, there are still those students who enjoy homework and the opportunity to complete it with their parent. Note to self and other educators: Be sure you provide choices of consequences that you can "live with," regardless of the choice the student selects. It's not alright to offer choices, and then change our minds when the student selects the option we didn't prefer. For example, if the student wishes to complete the work that evening as homework, we've got to be prepared to accept that (at least, the first time) and give the student the opportunity to follow through. That choice may no longer be an option for students who don't follow up with work completion at home, and it becomes necessary to offer another choice in future situations.

Using When/This Statements

As I discussed in the Expectations section, I know educators who utilize the If/Then statements to also communicate consequences for various misbehaviors. The problem I have experienced with my students is that they often view that "If you do not complete your work, then you will miss recess time" as an opportunity to engage in a power struggle with the teacher. In addition, if the teacher is utilizing

If/Then statements to communicate expectations, it can become confusing to use them for consequences as well.

One idea is to communicate the consequences of their actions is to use When/This Statements. For example, "Billy, **when** you continue to blurt out without raising a quiet hand, **this** may result in you losing the opportunity to join our discussion." It is my belief that, when presented with this type of vocabulary, the expectation is very clear as well as the consequence without it sounding like "you'd better follow the rules or else."

A chart outlining the differences between Logical & Illogical Consequences can be found in the Resources section.

Examples of When/This Statements can be found in the Resources section.

Hopeful
Hearts
Consequences
Accountability
Expectations
Relationships

"One year, I decided my classroom needed to be filled with a sense of hope; hope that this year, each student could be successful! I made posters with mottos saying, 'If you don't know the answer, we'll figure it out together' and 'It's only failure if you give up.' I made them myself because I wanted the students to notice, right away, that they were different than the store-bought posters, hopefully demonstrating immediately that they were important to me! Because I've learned that if it's important to the teacher, it becomes important to the students that respect you as well!"

Belinda Adams,
Don't Look Too Closely, 2018

Hopeful Hearts = Happy Classroom

"Happiness seems to have a positive effect on children's learning, memory, and social behavior. It is believed that positive mood states induce higher levels of activation and faster and more efficient information-processing strategies".
Vail, 1995

Some might wonder, how can I tell if I have a class of students with hopeful hearts and a happy classroom?

Hopeful, happy students have been known to laugh at their own mistakes, pointing it out to others and no longer feeling shame or frustration at their mistakes. Hopeful, happy students help one another when they see a peer is struggling with a word in the passage. Hopeful, happy students come to school each day ready to learn and are excited to share their knowledge with others.

To be certain, I rely on the words from my students in order to gauge how well we are doing in accomplishing this goal.

Statements of hopeful, happy students:

"I love school."

"I couldn't wait to be here today!"

"I love you."

"You're the best teacher."

"This is the bestest year I've ever had!"

"My mom is gonna be so proud. I can't wait to show her what I did."

One 1st grade student I'd had in class over 10 years previously contacted me when he graduated from high school. After we'd discussed what he'd done since I'd last seen him, he reminded me of all the fun we had in 1st grade. When I asked, what did he recall, I was pleasantly surprised to hear he remembered a great deal.

He remembered our daily "Hokey Pokey" before lunch, the read-alouds after lunch to a bunch of kids who had never heard a story read aloud before, and our daily afternoon release to "Who Let the Dogs Out?" He laughed and said, "I'm pretty sure we were the only class in the whole school who left every day barking!" Well, he's probably right about that.

These are the lasting memories I hope to leave behind in my wake of papers, lessons, and lists of all I need to do for the next day.

You may wonder why I place such high value on the idea of instilling our students with hope. I guess it depends a great deal on the students you have in your class. For students of poverty, hope shows them that the glass can be half full and teaches them how to enjoy the last half of the drink without worrying about when there will be more. For students of trauma, hope provides them with a glimpse into a future that doesn't involve shame, pain, failure, and discouragement. For other students, providing them with hope builds upon the tools they already have to make them experience more success in school.

> *"Motivation starts with an idea and a hope, gathers momentum to sustain a plan".*
>
> Vail, 1994, p. 7.

A class of hopeful students will transform your classroom into a happy place to be and an effective learning environment! Learning is no longer a chore, but rather a challenge they readily accept. On days when the work is challenging, students fall back on their relationships with their teacher and peers to help them achieve what they might see as too difficult on their own. Further, these same classrooms become examples for other classrooms to follow.

Whether or not students become lifelong learners and view learning as something they enjoy has a great deal of impact on their future choices in life. Hopeful students seek to get better and better at tasks, such as reading and math. Hopeful students take personal and academic risks because they feel supported. Hopeful students build relationships that teach them the positives of working as a team of learners. Hopeful students look to the future and see the possibility of college and their future careers.

Isn't that what all educators are striving for? Cultivating that lifelong learner in each of our students.

Wrapping Up

"...think about <u>who</u> you teach and more importantly, <u>how</u> your teaching will influence <u>who</u> they are."
Angela Maiers, Habitudes, 2012

At the end of the day, when all papers have been graded (okay, I'm kidding) and you've made copies for the following day, don't all of us want to look back and recall a room of students who went home with proud smiles of accomplishment and a desire to return tomorrow? Further, if you're like me, you'd also like to affirm yourself that you've done your best to teach them a life skill they can take with them from your class to another classroom and into their adulthood. Learning to understand the value of relationships, the need for expectations and accountability, and that there are consequences for our actions are invaluable life skills that will never lose their importance in students' future lives.

Refer to my triangle again. Those components weren't arranged so that they would spell the word, R-E-A-C-H. They were placed that way because, without developing them in this logical order with the appropriate weight given to each section, classrooms will continue to be places where students are disengaged or unruly, growth is minimal, and teachers are exhausted from their daily struggles to instruct.

Many teachers over the years have said, "I wish I had your magic formula. Your kids work so hard and they're respectful." To that, I usually respond with a proud smile – but not pride in myself, pride in a group of kids who have chosen to overcome their individual challenges, to open their hearts to relationships, to open their minds to new experiences, and to accomplish more learning than they ever thought possible.

Prior to writing this book, I'd often try to launch into a description of the 4 essentials of classroom success. Once I'd made it through the first two, I'd frequently see an expression on the teacher's face that said, "never mind" or "how do you find time to do all of that?" Now, I can eagerly hand them a copy of this quick reference book with the hopes that they, too, might discover the "magic formula" to classroom success that leads to great student growth and a happy classroom for all.

Resources

Expectations

Sample pages from beginning of the day Social Story:

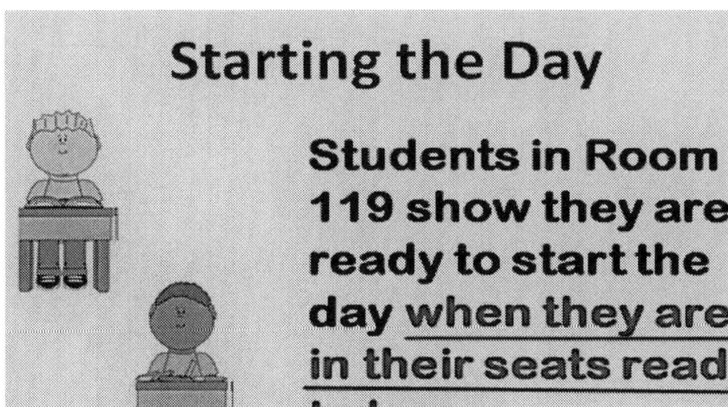

Accountability

Checklist to complete before raising hand for help from the teacher:

Check ✓	Action
	1. Have I read the directions again?
	2. Have I underlined or highlighted key parts of the directions?
	3. Is there a resource on the wall I can use to help me do this work?
	4. Is there work I have done before that is similar that will help me complete this work?

Sample motivational poster mottos you can create:

"It's only failure if you give up."

"If you don't know the answer, we will find out together."

"Nothing is easy to do until you practice."

"Be the person that makes you happy."

"You only lose the race if you stop running."

Classroom Expectations Chart

Expectation	Student Behavior	Steps to Correct
Show you are ready for learning by sitting in your seat	Students do not go to their seats; students slouch in chairs or put heads down on the desk	• Define the problem of the behavior. • Demonstrate a "ready to learn" posture looks and explain its importance. • Practice the "ready to learn" posture. • Develop non-verbal cues. • Practice role-modeling. • Set clear consequences for continuing behavior.
Raise hand to speak	Students blurt out; students talk over one another	• Define the problem of the behavior. • Set clear expectations. • Acknowledge positive efforts. • Develop non-verbal cues. • Practice role-modeling. • Set clear consequences for continuing behavior.
Raise hand to get out of seat	Students get up without permission; students wander classroom; students disturb other students	• Define the problem of the behavior. • Set clear expectations. • Develop consistent classroom routines that allow for movement breaks. • Provide opportunities for sensory breaks. • Acknowledge positive efforts. • Carefully consider and reconsider seat arrangement / make changes. • Develop non-verbal cues. • Practice role-modeling. • Set clear consequences for continuing behavior.
Listen for directions and follow them when asked the first time	Students do not follow directions; students ask for directions to be repeated multiple times; students refuse to work or do not complete their work	• Define the problem of the behavior. • Use language in your directions that is appropriate to the skill set of the students. • Develop consistent methods for delivering directions & writing them on board. • Acknowledge positive efforts. • Utilize strategies for individual students, such as directions on post-its or written at the top of their paper for reminders. • Determine when to ignore non-compliance or address. • Set clear consequences for continuing behavior.
Let us help you when you need assistance	Students refuse teacher help; students become angry because they are not sure what to do/how to do it; students act out in inappropriate ways	• Define the problem of the behavior. • Provide levels of support that students know and understand. • Offer different forms of assistance to meet individual student needs. • Offer assistance quietly so as not to embarrass student. • Know when student is too angry to accept help and prompt student to "take a break".

Expectations

If/Then Statement Sample Chart

If	**Then**
If you sit and raise a quiet hand,	Then I will come and help you.
If you finish your morning work,	Then you can take a brain break.
If you are ready to work,	Then get out your supplies and show you are ready to work.
If you are feeling frustrated,	Then ask for help or ask to take a quick break.
If you would like to share your story,	Then raise a quiet hand and I will be happy to call on you.

Sample of an Interest Survey

~Interest Survey~

Name: ________________________________
Date: _________________________________

When I am not at school, my favorite activity is to _______________________________________.

If I could select one item from home and bring it to school, it would be ______________________ because _________________________________.

When I am at school, one thing I think about that makes me happy is _________________________ ____.

When I finish all of my class work, one activity that I would love to do is __________________ ____.

If that wasn't possible, the next best thing would be to __________________________________.

Consequences

When/This Statements for Communicating Consequences

When	This
When you continue to blurt out answers without raising a quiet hand,	This may result in you losing the opportunity to join us in the discussion.
When you continue to ignore the classroom expectation to work quietly without disturbing others,	This may cause you to lose some points on your point sheet or have to make up this tin during free time.
When your behavior disrupts the learning of others,	This becomes a problem for the whole class and will result in a consequence.
When you do not let me know you are confused about how to complete the work,	This leads me to believe you are choosing not to complete the work and doesn't let me know you need help.

Note: Take student age and circumstances into account when determining complexity of vocabulary used; however, don't underestimate the ability to comprehend, even by your youngest students.

Comparison of Logical & Illogical Consequences

Behavior	**Logical consequence**	**Illogical consequence**
Yelling out answers	Leaving the group	Loss of recess
Disrupting the learning of others	Short timeout in calm down area	Suspension from school
Being disrespectful to adults	Short letter of apology or personal apology	Staying after school
Being unsafe with a pencil	Writing with a crayon for a given time	Sent away from work table
Being unsafe on the swings	Loss of swing privileges for a given time	Stand by the wall at recess
Note: Take student age and circumstances into account when determining length of consequence.		

This chart originally appeared in If Only She Knew, 2019.

Or email Anchor Book Press, Ltd for a free downloadable PDF.

Anchorbookpress@gmail.com

REACH for Success

4 Strategies to Positively Impact Your Classroom

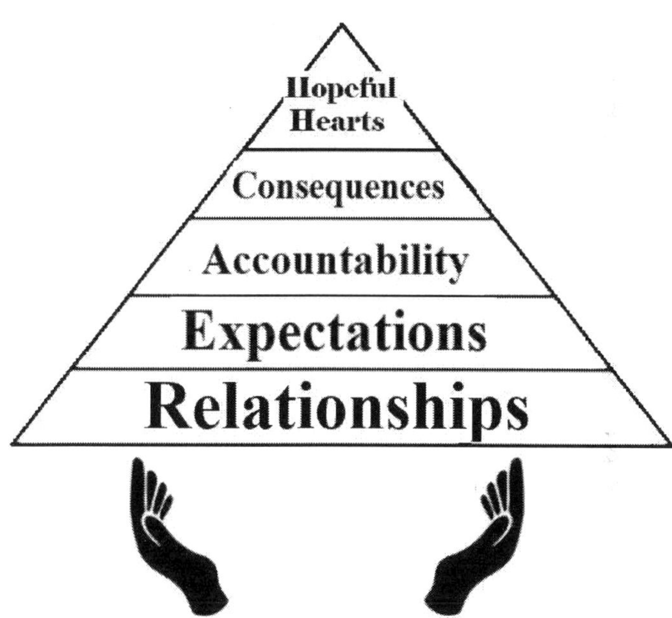

Reflection of Book Concepts and Implementation Guide

Reflecting on the strategies presented in this book, what are your overall thoughts about using these components to increase your classroom success?

____

____

____

____

Which of the components do you feel you already include in your daily classroom management and instruction? How successful do you feel they are in assisting your students to be available for learning?

____

____

____

____

____

Which component(s) do you feel you do not include in your daily classroom management and instruction? How might you add those component(s) to your classroom management to improve classroom behavior and increase student academic success?

____

____

____

____

____

Reflecting on your recent classes over the past few years, which strategy do you think would have improved your classroom climate? How might you begin to implement that component?

____

____

____

____

____

When explaining expectations, how might utilizing the If/Then Statements assist you?

____

____

____

____

What statements might you add to the chart that fits your classroom management style?

If	**Then**
If you sit and raise a quiet hand,	Then I will come and help you.
If you finish your morning work,	Then you can take a brain break.
If you are ready to work,	Then get out your supplies and show you are ready to work.
If you are feeling frustrated,	Then ask for help or ask to take a quick break.
If you would like to share your story,	Then raise a quiet hand and I will be happy to call on you.

Reflecting on consequences, both logical and illogical, what ideas can you add to the chart:

Behavior	**Logical consequence**	**Illogical consequence**
Yelling out answers	Leaving the group	Loss of recess
Disrupting the learning of others	Short timeout in calm down area	Suspension from school
Being disrespectful to adults	Short letter of apology or personal apology	Staying after school
Being unsafe with a pencil	Writing with a crayon for a given time	Sent away from work table
Being unsafe on the swings	Loss of swing privileges for a given time	Stand by the wall at recess
Note: Take student age and circumstances into account when determining length of consequence.		

This chart originally appeared in If Only She Knew Implementation Guide, 2019.

Thinking about the use of When/This Statements, how might you be able to utilize them in the classroom?

____

____

____

____

How might you add onto the chart below to include specific statements that apply to your unique classroom and students?

When	**This**
When you continue to blurt out answers without raising a quiet hand,	This may result in you losing the opportunity to join us in the discussion.
When you continue to ignore the classroom expectation to work quietly without disturbing others,	This may cause you to lose some points on your point sheet or have to make up this time during free time.
When your behavior disrupts the learning of others,	This becomes a problem for the whole class and will result in a consequence.
When you do not let me know you are confused about how to complete the work,	This leads me to believe you are choosing not to complete the work and doesn't let me know you need help.

What are your over-riding thoughts on the impact these strategies might have on your classroom as a whole?

____

____

____

____

How might implementing them benefit your class?

____

____

____

____

What reservations do you have about implementing them? Do you see your reservations as outweighing the possible positive effects?

____

____

____

If you are struggling with the time commitment that implementation of these strategies may require, how might you break them up in order to fit them into your day? Better yet. Is there a teacher you could team-teach with who could assist you in introducing the strategies?

____

____

____

____

If you attempted any of the strategies, what was the impact on your classroom? Did you see the value in taking the time to implement them?

____

____

____

____

____

____

What suggestions/comments would you like to share with the author, Belinda Adams, about the strategies presented in this book?

____

____

____

____

____

____

Visit Belinda's Facebook page
Teachers *REACH for Success*
and message her with your
thoughts and feedback!
She'd love to share them on her page.

Bibliography

Adams, Belinda. Don't Look Too Closely: What Students of Trauma are Hiding and How You Can be the Difference for Them. Anchor Book Press, Ltd., Palatine, IL, 2018.

Adams, Belinda. If Only She Knew: Engaging the Whole Student with Trauma in Mind. Anchor Book Press, Ltd., Palatine, IL, 2019.

Benson, Jeffrey. Hanging In: Strategies for Teaching the Students Who Challenge Us Most. ASCD, Alexandria, VA, 2014.

Fay, Jim & Funk, David. Teaching with Love and Logic: Taking Control of the Classroom. The Love & Logic Institute, Inc. Golden, CO, 1995.

George, John & George, Rachael. 10 Strategies and Practices That Can Help All Students Overcome Barriers. ASCD.org. http://inservice.ascd.org/author/admin/, 2016.

Maiers, Angela. Classroom Habitudes: Teaching Habits and Attitudes for 21st Century Learning, Solution Tree Press, Bloomington, IN, 2012.

Vail, Priscilla L. Emotion: The On / Off Switch for Learning, Walker and Company, New York, NY, 1994.

Books by Belinda Adams

Can You See Me? Using Understanding to Help Students of Poverty Feel Seen, Heard & Valued in the Classroom

Can you See Me? is a book for educators, administrators and just about anyone else who wants to understand why students of poverty are struggling in today's white, middle-class educational model. Belinda Adams does a great job of explaining cultural differences and how educators can use this knowledge to change the classroom into a place where all children feel seen and understood. Years of success working with students of poverty have given Belinda a clear picture of what works and what doesn't. Read this light-hearted and informative book, full of stories that will make you laugh and make you cry.

Winner of the
Blue Ribbon Award

*The **D300 Blue Ribbon Society** comprises a select group of distinguished members who epitomize District 300's values. The Society aims to recognize their greatness and celebrate their achievements*

Don't Look Too Closely: What Students of Trauma are Hiding in the Classroom and How You Can be the Difference for Them

Don't Look Too Closely challenges educators to turn an observing eye at their students, seeking to discover what they are hiding. When children hide trauma, it's generally for a variety of reasons; however, the effect of this trauma impacts their availability for learning in debilitating ways. When statistics show that one in four children have experienced a traumatic event, educators cannot turn a blind eye on the negative impact on these children's lives but also how this trauma influences the effectiveness of instruction and the overall classroom climate. In this book, Belinda discusses the negative effect of trauma on both the younger and older child. Belinda's book is for educators, administrators and anyone who wants to know what to look for, how to begin to understand what's unfathomable to most, and how to use what you know to help these children be more successful in the classroom and life.

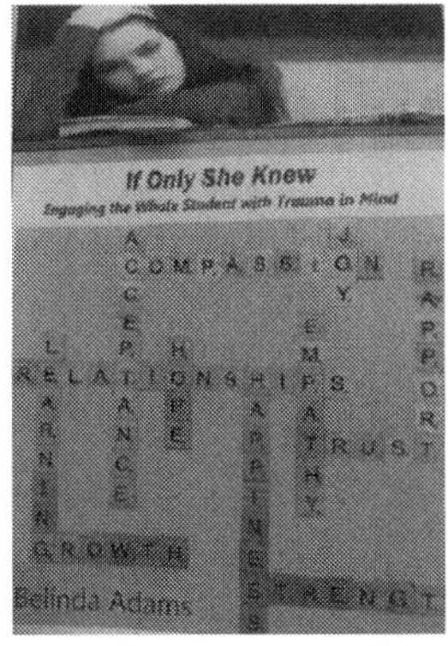

If Only She Knew: Engaging the Whole Student with Trauma in Mind

Trauma does not discriminate. The lasting effects that trauma brings into a child's life applies to all students of all demographics, varying financial status, culture and different family dynamics. Trauma has impacted the lives of 1 out of 4 children. Chances are you have one of these children in your classroom or school today. Teachers are in a unique situation to positively impact the lives of children living with trauma, perhaps making the difference that helps them see their future with hope. After a special unit on Heroes, one of Belinda's students wrote: "I want to think that a hero can be anyone. But I see the bad that some people do. I want to be the kind of person someone thinks of as a hero." Showing students to view their situation as hopeful can make you a hero to a child of trauma.

Why MATH: Engaging At-Risk Students in Math and Science When the Teacher Hates Teaching It

What if every teacher who taught mathematics or science was a gifted mathematician or a scientist? All students would excel in these elite fields of academics! However, few educators would attest to gifted status in math and science or even if those subjects make their creative juices flow. There are other educators who find those subjects disengaging and perhaps a bit intimidating. This book is dedicated to those educators who feel more comfortable dealing with nouns, verbs and run-on sentences. Yet, with careful planning and implementation, every educator can deliver effective instruction in math and science.

Future Books by Belinda Adams

Throw Away Kids

When most see those three words, it is the low-income and foster care situations that probably come to mind first. That is NOT what this book is about. Special education colleagues and diligent advocates for students with special needs, Carol Pirog and Belinda Adams, collaborate as they jump onto the slippery slope of issues plaguing students labeled as needing "special education".

Breaking protocols of what might be considered "politically correct", Carol and Belinda shed light on who these *Throw Away Kids* are and our obligation, as educators and parents, to turn the tide in their favor. *Throw Away Kids* are kids of every ethnicity and income range. They are the kids that need advocates to help them find their own voices and empower them as they move toward success.

Can You See Me Yet?

A follow-up book to her best-selling book on teaching students of poverty. Belinda continues to strive to challenge herself and her students to be successful in the classroom, not just academically but emotionally as well.

Her candid stories about her students of poverty demonstrate the increasing number of students of poverty in our classrooms and the need to develop specific strategies that motivate them to want to come to school and participate actively in the learning process.

With her many years of experience in teaching at schools where 97% of the students qualified for "free or reduced lunches," and where breakfast is served each day in the classroom before learning can begin, Belinda's approaches demonstrate that, with diligence and awareness, teachers can help these struggling students achieve academic success and hopefully a lifetime of success!

About the Author

Belinda Adams is an elementary teacher. In addition to many years of experience in the classroom, she has degrees in elementary education, special education, and psychology. She has taught students in kindergarten through eighth grade, encompassing general education students, students in special education, and students in regular education who needed remediation.

Belinda is the author of *Can You See Me? Using Understanding to Help Students of Poverty Feel Seen, Heard and Valued in the Classroom, Don't Look Too Closely: What Children of Trauma are Hiding and How You Can be the Difference for Them,* and *If Only She Knew: Engaging the Whole Student with Trauma in Mind*. Her books are based on her experiences in the classroom. She also wrote *Why Math? Mental Anguish to Humanity: Engaging At-Risk Students in Math and Science When the Teacher Hates Teaching It.*

With success rates that exceed expected yearly growth, Belinda is always available to discuss solutions for dealing with difficult students because she believes every student *wants* to learn when given the right motivation and support.

Before becoming a teacher, Belinda worked in the business world and wrote a weekly editorial for a northwestern Illinois newspaper. In her spare time, oh wait, Belinda is a teacher and an author, she doesn't have spare time. She lives in the Midwest with her husband, her son, and her dogs, Murphy & Suzy Q.

Visit Belinda on her Author page on Amazon or her Facebook page, *Teachers REACH for Success, Belinda Adams.*

Index of Key Terms

Notes:

Made in the USA
Monee, IL
20 January 2020